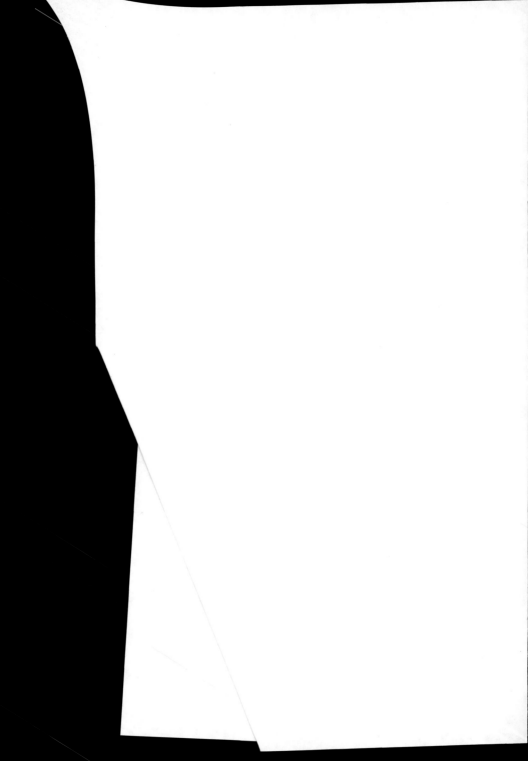

Intercessions for Daily Prayer

Simon Pothen is Canon Precentor
of Chelmsford Cathedral

Intercessions for Daily Prayer

Simon Pothen

CANTERBURY
PRESS
Norwich

I would like to dedicate this book to the memory of my dear parents, the Reverend Prebendary John Pothen and Florrie Pothen; to my dear brother Philip; and to my wife Deb, and my children Joshua, Abigail, Bethany, Martha and Noah.

© Simon Pothen 2009

First published in 2009 by the Canterbury Press Norwich
Editorial office
13–17 Long Lane,
London, EC1A 9PN, UK

Canterbury Press is an imprint of Hymns Ancient and Modern Ltd
(a registered charity)
St Mary's Works, St Mary's Plain,
Norwich, NR3 3BH, UK

www.scm-canterburypress.co.uk

British Library Cataloguing in Publication data

A catalogue record for this book is available
from the British Library

978 1 85311 961 3

Typeset by Regent Typesetting, London
Printed and bound in Great Britain by
CPI Antony Rowe, Chippenham, Wiltshire

Contents

Acknowledgements

I would like to thank the Dean and Chapter of Chelmsford Cathedral for the generous giving of time for this book; their help, support and prayers are much appreciated. I owe thanks and gratitude to the Benedictine Community of Alton Abbey, where I have deep joy of being an oblate, and to the Parish and people of St. John the Baptist Church, Pinner. Finally I would like to thank my wife Deb and my children for their unstinting encouragement and love. I would like to take this opportunity to thank Christine Smith, Mary Matthews and all the staff at Canterbury Press who have helped with the publication of this book.

Foreword

Some of us are old enough to remember the Book of Common Prayer as the only liturgical resource available for both eucharistic and other worship. Intercession at the Eucharist was the 'Prayer for the Church Militant' and at the office provision was through the collects and the 'Prayers and Thanksgivings' which followed. Through the *Alternative Service Book* and more particularly through *Common Worship* a whole new world has opened up for all. Indeed there are now courses for lay intercessors at the eucharist and supplementary material available.

For the office, much of the earlier material was available in the form of more collects. The rich material produced by Eric Milner White and G. W. Briggs especially comes to mind. With the enrichment of the office in *Common Worship: Daily Prayer*, however, there arises a still greater need for imaginative intercession material to be made available. It is easy for 'the daily pray-er' to become wearied with the need to intercede anew with fresh voice every day. Simon Pothen's excellent book speaks directly to this need. His material, including litany-style responses and rich intercessory reflection, offers us all just the sort of supplementary texts that will assist us in our daily praying. Simon has effectively supplemented the *Common Worship* library but has done so with an independence of mind that complements the official provision. His work is something for

which we should be profoundly grateful and which I hope will
be widely used.

+Stephen Wakefield
Chairman, Church of England Liturgical Commission

Introduction

Twenty years ago when I was ordained, the *Alternative Service Book 1980* had been bedded down in the consciousness of the Church of England and was being used for the Daily Offices in the parish where I served my title. I can remember this discipline being a trial at best and a bit of a bore at worst. There was little awareness that this was a time of prayer. I don't think I was alone in feeling this. When *Common Worship: Daily Prayer* was published in 2005 a new era opened up: the variety of texts, the dedication to the liturgical seasons and the fresh translations of the psalms have truly given us a real prayer book.

Intercessions for Daily Prayer is an attempt to provide daily intercessions for those for whom the discipline of the Daily Office is non-negotiable. This book arose out of a particularly barren patch in my own prayers; I felt that my intercessions were becoming more and more personal and less and less about the Church, the Church's year, the world and my own community. Prayer in this context can become stilted, withdrawn and entirely subjective, and it was during one of these spells that I felt the need to address wider issues in the life of the Church and the world. So the seed of this book was sown.

The book has been written to be used at the Daily Office, though it can also be used for the Daily Eucharist. I would like to think that its breadth, flexibility and brevity allow it to be used for both and, indeed, wherever there is a need for intercession, whether it be before a meeting, at a Bible study or a house group or any occasion.

We are all prone to periods of barrenness and times when our intercessions become dry, and this book is offered to enable the priest and the layperson to pray with the Church, using the liturgical seasons as the wellspring of prayer and intercession. I hope people will find the material here both helpful and prayerful.

Simon Pothen
Advent 2008

Advent Season

Sundays to Saturdays

Sundays

Come to us, Lord Jesus, we thirst for you and long for your gracious love to be shown to us. Come to us and hear our longings and desires.

Lord our God, prepare your people for the coming of your Son: in eager hope we pray,
come, Lord Jesus, do not delay.

Guide your Church through the ministry of wise and holy leaders, be with N our bishop and bless the ministry of all bishops: in eager hope we pray,
come, Lord Jesus, do not delay.

You will come in judgement and power. May your just and gentle rule reign in the lives of all who hold authority: in eager hope we pray,
come, Lord Jesus, do not delay.

We remember and bring before you, O Lord, all who through their work strive to make the world a better place to live in.

Shower upon all of us the needful gifts of grace and love: in eager hope we pray,
come, Lord Jesus, do not delay.

Bless this parish, our life and our witness; guide us during this season of Advent. Enable us to work for your kingdom ....:
in eager hope we pray,
come, Lord Jesus, do not delay.

In your mercy and love look upon those who suffer. We pray for .... Restore them and raise them up so that all your children may share in the glory that you have promised: in eager hope we pray,
come, Lord Jesus, do not delay.

Mondays

In you, O Lord, we put our trust; in your steadfast love hear us.

Increase in us a sense of expectancy as we wait with eager long-ing for your rule of justice and mercy: come and reign in our hearts, O Lord,
may your kingdom come.

Pour into the hearts of all who hold authority in our church the spirit of knowledge and the fear of the Lord ....: come and reign in our hearts, O Lord,
may your kingdom come.

We long for your rule of justice and mercy: come and reign in our hearts, O Lord,
may your kingdom come.

Bless those who campaign for the rights of all oppressed people:
come and reign in our hearts, O Lord,
may your kingdom come.

We pray for the schools of our parish .... Be with all pupils, head teachers, governors, staff and parents. Enable us to work together for our children's education and nurture: come and reign in our hearts, O Lord,
may your kingdom come.

Hear the cries of those who are broken and live in the shadow of despair. May they find hope and healing in you, the source of all love: come and reign in our hearts, O Lord,
may your kingdom come.

Tuesdays

Make ready our hearts and minds, through prayer, to wait expectantly for the coming of Jesus Christ. May we go out to meet him when he appears.

Prepare our hearts to welcome you, O Lord. May we hear the message of John the Baptist anew: come to us, O Lord,
come and visit your people.

Bless all who guide and lead our Church .... Fill them with your truth and love: come to us, O Lord,
come and visit your people.

Convert us your children; direct our hearts and wills to serve you in serving others: come to us, O Lord,
come and visit your people.

As John the Baptist hungered and thirsted for your righteousness and justice, stir in our hearts that same hunger to see your will prevail in the world: come to us, O Lord,
come and visit your people.

Be with all those who are responsible for the hospitals in our area .... We pray for all who are sick, in particular .... and for those who care ....: come to us, O Lord,
come and visit your people.

You will not break the broken reed nor put out the dimly burning wick. Enable us to minister with compassion in your world: come to us, O Lord,
come and visit your people.

Wednesdays

Hear our prayers, O Lord; set alight our hearts with the promise of your glory.

Bless us during this season of Advent, that we will be ready for your coming among us: maranatha,
come, Lord Jesus.

Enable all Christian leaders to preach and teach the gospel. We pray for N our bishop. Confirm your ministers in your truth and pour upon them the gifts of your Holy Spirit: maranatha,
come, Lord Jesus.

May all nations be subject to your just and gentle rule: maranatha,
come, Lord Jesus.

We pray for all who keep your Church aware of the needs of your suffering children and for all who work for their relief: maranatha,
come, Lord Jesus.

We pray for all who work in commerce, particularly those whose work is in our parish .... We remember those whose work is hard and unrewarding: maranatha,
come, Lord Jesus.

Spread your healing love on all who live in despair. Comfort them with your peace and love: maranatha,
come, Lord Jesus.

Thursdays

You are our help and our salvation; come, Lord, do not delay.

Stir in our hearts the eagerness that longs for your birth: come among us,
and visit us, your children.

Come and pour your love into the hearts of all the leaders of your Church; fill them with wisdom: come among us,
and visit us, your children.

Bless all who hold authority, that they may know your will and desire for all your children: come among us,
and visit us, your children.

We remember those who are alert to the needs of your children who live in the shadow of injustice and hatred: come among us,
and visit us, your children.

Pour your love and grace upon all who work for our local authority .... We pray for those who provide services to people in need .... come among us,
and visit us, your children.

Come and show your power to those who are broken by the experiences of life. Reveal your love and compassion to them: come among us,
and visit us, your children.

Fridays

The appointed time is near, may we reject the works of darkness and put on the armour of light. As we come to you in prayer, may the purity of your light shine into our hearts.

Help us to realize that our salvation is near. Prepare our hearts and minds for your coming: come wisdom from on high,
and be near us, Lord.

Bless N our bishop and all church leaders. Enable them to reflect more fully the love and compassion of Jesus: come wisdom from on high,
and be near us, Lord.

We pray for people who live in the shadow of darkness, in countries where authority is abused and human rights denied. May your light shine courageously in the hearts of all who endure oppression and danger: come wisdom from on high,
and be near us, Lord.

We pray for organizations that work for children who need our

help .... May their love and advocacy shine brightly in the darkness of this world: come wisdom from on high,
and be near us, Lord.

Hold in the palm of your hand all those who hold authority in our local council .... We pray for N *(and N)* our local councillor(s) and N our MP. Enable them to serve you in serving all your children: come wisdom from on high,
and be near us, Lord.

May your light shine in the hearts of those whose lives are marred by despair and anxiety ....: come wisdom from on high,
and be near us, Lord.

Saturdays

Our salvation is near and glory will dwell in our land. So in faithful obedience we come to you in prayer.

Enable your Church to be faithful to the will of God. Strengthen her obedience: Son of Mary,
come to us in your love.

Guard and guide all our bishops .... May they hold before them the example of our Lord Jesus Christ, the Shepherd of souls: Son of Mary,
come to us in your love.

Protect this and every nation. May those in authority be obedient to your will and serve you faithfully as they serve all your children: Son of Mary,
come to us in your love.

Teach us the way of your commands, O Lord, that we may serve the needs of justice in the world: Son of Mary,
come to us in your love.

We give thanks for our own witness in this parish .... We give thanks for the partnerships that we have forged that witness to the love you have for the world: Son of Mary,
come to us in your love.

We remember the broken-hearted .... Enable us to serve them: Son of Mary,
come to us in your love.

Advent between December 17 and 24

December 17 O Sapientia – *O Wisdom*

O Divine Wisdom, come into our hearts and pour on us the spirit of discernment, that this time of prayer may be sanctified by the gracious covering of your wings.

You are near, O Lord Christ. Keep us faithful in our watching and our waiting: O Wisdom from on high,
come and teach us the way of truth.

Bless and guide our bishops, particularly *N* our bishop. Consecrate them in your truth: O Wisdom from on high,
come and teach us the way of truth.

Bless our nation. May this season of waiting be a time of discerning the true value of life: O Wisdom from on high,
come and teach us the way of truth.

Give courage and patience to all those who strive for justice and peace in our world: O Wisdom from on high,
come and teach us the way of truth.

We pray for this parish in bearing witness to you .... Give us grace and courage that we may wait in loving confidence for your coming: O Wisdom from on high,
come and teach us the way of truth.

Guide and protect those who are vulnerable, and those whose lives are shattered by betrayal. Come, O Lord, with your healing wings: O Wisdom from on high,
come and teach us the way of truth.

December 18 O Adonai – O *Almighty Lord*

O Adonai, set our hearts ablaze with the fire of your love. May this time of prayer teach us your law.

Guard and bless your Church. May we be found ready when our Lord appears: leader of your people,
come in your might and power.

Bless our bishops, particularly N our bishop. Give them grace to be good and wise pastors of your children: leader of your people,
come in your might and power.

Guide and bless all those who hold authority among the nations of the world. May their authority be exercised with wisdom and discernment: leader of your people,
come in your might and power.

Defend with your mighty presence those who are peacemakers in your world: leader of your people,
come in your might and power.

Inspire with your love and knowledge all those who work to inspire our children's learning. We pray for our local schools .... and for all who are entrusted with the care and protection of our children: leader of your people,
come in your might and power.

Mend those whose lives are broken by sickness, sadness and despair ....: leader of your people,
come in your might and power.

December 19 O Radix Jesse – *O Root of Jesse*

O Root of Jesse, we fall silent in prayer, for you are God. Embrace us in your arms.

Prepare your Church, O Lord, with the promise of your coming. That we may offer you a fitting sacrifice of praise: we fall silent before you, O Lord,
come and deliver us! Do not delay!

Protect your Church through wise and holy pastors. Bless *N* our bishop: we fall silent before you, O Lord,
come and deliver us! Do not delay!

Bless all nations. We remember those nations caught up in war and disaster. May your almighty power rule in the hearts of all those who hold authority: we fall silent before you, O Lord,
come and deliver us! Do not delay!

Guard and defend all those who work to establish peace in the hearts of your children: we fall silent before you, O Lord,
come and deliver us! Do not delay!

Heal all those whose lives are scarred by sickness ………. Bless those who care for the sick and give them patience and a loving heart: we fall silent before you, O Lord,
come and deliver us! Do not delay!

December 20 O Clavis David – *O Key of David*

O Key of David, open our hearts and banish the deeds of darkness, so that this time of prayer may be blessed by the light of your presence.

Enliven us, O Lord, with the promise of your coming. Give us patience during this time: come and lead us,
and free us from the darkness.

Inspire all who lead the Church. We pray for *N* our bishop: come and lead us,
and free us from the darkness.

Bless and guide all who govern the nations. May they exercise their power for the common good of all your children: come and lead us,
and free us from the darkness.

Protect with your gracious presence those who work for peace in a dangerous and violent world: come and lead us,
and free us from the darkness.

Bless those who work in our shops and in the small businesses of this parish ....: come and lead us,
and free us from the darkness.

Comfort with your healing touch all those whose lives are scarred by despair: come and lead us,
and free us from the darkness.

December 21 O Oriens – O *Rising Sun*

O Rising Sun, enlighten us with your presence, warm our hearts with your healing touch so that our prayers may be a fitting sacrifice of thanksgiving and love.

Enlighten your Church with the promise of the coming joy: splendour of eternal light,
come and enlighten us.

Guide our bishops with your truth. We pray particularly for N our bishop: splendour of eternal light,
come and enlighten us.

Bless all leaders. Give them a desire to serve you in serving their people: splendour of eternal light,
come and enlighten us.

Enfold in your love all those who work for peace and justice in our world: splendour of eternal light,
come and enlighten us.

Bless those who work to provide leisure services in this local authority ....: splendour of eternal light,
come and enlighten us.

Enlighten the hearts of those who are facing the darkness of brokenness and despair: splendour of eternal light,
come and enlighten us.

December 22 O Rex Gentium – *O King of the People*

O King of the People, the desire of nations and hope of all people, hear our prayer which we bring before you.

Unite your Church, preserve her in truth and liberate her to serve you: reign in our hearts, O Lord,
come and save us.

Bless and guide our bishops. We pray for N our bishop: reign in our hearts, O Lord,
come and save us.

Inspire the leaders of the nations with the vision of your just and gentle rule: reign in our hearts, O Lord,
come and save us.

Defend with your mighty power those who work for justice and peace in our world: reign in our hearts, O Lord,
come and save us.

Strengthen and defend all those who hold authority in our local area .... We pray for our mayor N and the officers of the council: reign in our hearts, O Lord,
come and save us.

Heal those whose lives are crushed and broken by despair and fear: reign in our hearts, O Lord,
come and save us.

December 23 O Emmanuel – *O God-with-us*

O Emmanuel, our king and judge, hear the prayers that we bring before you; in your mercy, hear the cries of our hearts.

We wait for your coming, Lord Jesus. May our hearts be prepared to greet your gentle rule: we wait for your loving kindness,
come and save us, O Lord.

Inspire our bishops with your gracious love. We pray for *N* our bishop: we wait for your loving kindness,
come and save us, O Lord.

May your rule inspire the hearts of all who hold authority: we wait for your loving kindness,
come and save us, O Lord.

May the promise of your birth guide and defend all those who work for justice in your world: we wait for your loving kindness,
come and save us, O Lord.

Pour your blessing upon this church; enable us to bring in your kingdom. Bless our work with children and young people ....: we wait for your loving kindness,
come and save us, O Lord.

Tend the vulnerable, protect the weak and bring your healing to those whose lives are scarred and broken: we wait for your loving kindness,
come and save us, O Lord.

December 24

We wait in prayer with eager longing for your incarnation. Come into the silence of our waiting and listen to our needs, prayers and longings.

Direct your Church into the way of truth and love: tomorrow the Lord will come,
and we shall see his glory.

Govern the hearts and minds of our bishops; bless them in their work. We pray for *N* our bishop: tomorrow the Lord will come,
and we shall see his glory.

Rule in the hearts of all who hold authority in the world: tomorrow the Lord will come,
and we shall see his glory.

Encourage those who work to establish your kingdom in the hearts of all your children: tomorrow the Lord will come,
and we shall see his glory.

Give healing to those whose lives are broken by despair and fear: tomorrow the Lord will come,
and we shall see his glory.

Christmas Season

Christmas Day to January 5

Sundays to Saturdays

Sundays

Word made flesh, glory of the Father, hope of our world. Hear our prayers and always show us your love.

For the dignity of all your children: we pray to you, O Lord,
save us through your birth.

For the Holy Land and for the peace of Jerusalem: we pray to you, O Lord,
save us through your birth.

For the dispossessed, the asylum-seeker and for all who seek refuge in our country: we pray to you, O Lord,
save us through your birth.

For those who have no shelter: we pray to you, O Lord,
save us through your birth.

For the work of our parish and our witness to the world ....:
we pray to you, O Lord,
save us through your birth.

For all families who will share in the joy of this season and for those for whom this season is a painful reminder of lost contacts: we pray to you, O Lord,
save us through your birth.

Mondays

In your mercy and love, hear the prayers of your people. Come to us and dispel the darkness of this world.

Bless your Church in places of conflict and pain. Help us to bear witness to your everlasting kingdom of peace and righteousness: Lord, give us your peace,
and bring us your salvation.

We pray for the Holy Land, for reconciliation among all peoples: Lord, give us your peace,
and bring us your salvation.

We pray for all who have been forced to leave their homes and seek refuge in strange and often hostile lands; in the midst of deep darkness, may your light shine: Lord, give us your peace,
and bring us your salvation.

In recalling the poverty of the Holy Family we pray for those who are homeless: Lord, give us your peace,
and bring us your salvation.

Pour your blessings on the schools of this area .... We pray for all who bear responsibility for the care and nurture of our children: Lord, give us your peace,
and bring us your salvation.

We pray for all families and for the joy of family life. Enable us to reach out in love to those who are lonely: Lord, give us your peace,
and bring us your salvation.

Tuesdays

Emmanuel, 'God with us', enter the hearts of your faithful people as we make our prayers to you.

We give thanks for the witness of Christians in places where there is war, famine and hatred. We pray for ....: your kingdom come, O Lord,
Emmanuel, come and save us.

We pray for the religious and civic leaders of the peoples of the Middle-East, for peace between Jews, Christians and Muslims: your kingdom come, O Lord,
Emmanuel, come and save us.

We pray for those who are stateless, those forced from their homes because of persecution: your kingdom come, O Lord,
Emmanuel, come and save us.

We pray for the homeless and destitute. Move us to compassion and to the action that speaks of your love for all people: your kingdom come, O Lord,
Emmanuel, come and save us.

Enfold in your love all who care for the sick, for local hospitals .... doctors' surgeries and health visitors: your kingdom come, O Lord,
Emmanuel, come and save us.

We pray for all families, for children who are orphaned, for those who are abused and those who are in care: your kingdom come, O Lord,
Emmanuel, come and save us.

Wednesdays

We bring our prayers and supplications to your manger throne. Hear our prayers, O Child of Bethlehem.

We bring before you the needs of all Christians who witness to your love in troubled parts of our world. We pray for ....:
glory to God in the highest,
and peace to us his children.

We pray for the land of our Lord's birth, for peace and reconciliation among all God's people: glory to God in the highest,
and peace to us his children.

We pray for refugees and those forced to seek asylum far from their homeland: glory to God in the highest,
and peace to us his children.

We pray for the homeless, and for all who work for their relief: glory to God in the highest,
and peace to us his children.

Keep in your watchful care all who work in our parish ....;
for shopkeepers, office-workers and business leaders ....
May their work be inspired by the ideals of serving the common good. Bless us in our partnerships and the contacts we strive to make: glory to God in the highest,
and peace to us his children.

We give thanks to God for the gift of family life and the joy of children. We remember those families who are torn apart; give them the simple love and unity of the manger: glory to God in the highest,
and peace to us his children.

Thursdays

Lord God, we are your children. Hear our prayers and move our hearts to deeds of love.

Sow the spirit of peace and love into the hearts of all who spread violence in our world. We pray for .... May your Church witness to the truth that we are all your children: let heaven sing,
and earth rejoice.

May all your children listen to the song of the angels promising peace on earth. We pray particularly for the peoples of Israel and Palestine: let heaven sing,
and earth rejoice.

Bring comfort and peace to all who are refugees and asylum-seekers. Stir our hearts to reach out with love and compassion: let heaven sing,
and earth rejoice.

Your heart was moved by outcasts and the poor: comfort the homeless. Be with us as we strive to herald your kingdom of peace and joy: let heaven sing,
and earth rejoice.

We pray for those who work for the local authority. We pray particularly for those who look after our environment ....
Teach us to take our local responsibilities more seriously: let heaven sing,
and earth rejoice.

Your Son was born into a human family and shared the joys of an earthly home; be with all families and may children find their homes to be places of security and love: let heaven sing,
and earth rejoice.

Fridays

Lord Jesus, enter into our hearts during this time of prayer; make your home in us so that our lives may reflect the purity of your life.

Give your Church gifts of grace to bear witness to your love in places of conflict and hatred. We pray for your Church in ....: child of Bethlehem,
may your birth bring us peace.

Pour out your Spirit upon all who hold authority. We pray especially at this time for the leaders of Israel and Palestine and for all who are entrusted with the responsibilities of peace-making: child of Bethlehem,
may your birth bring us peace.

Give us your wisdom and love so that we may reach out with love and compassion to those who seek asylum and refugee status in this country: child of Bethlehem,
may your birth bring us peace.

Babe of Bethlehem, born in poverty, be with those who are homeless. Stir our hearts and move us to deeds of love: child of Bethlehem,
may your birth bring us peace.

Lord of heaven and earth, rule in the hearts of all who hold authority. We pray for our local councillors .... and for our MP .... child of Bethlehem,
may your birth bring us peace.

Bless all families with your grace and truth. Encourage parents and children alike to share a deep and lasting love: child of Bethlehem,
may your birth bring us peace.

Saturdays

Your word sustains all things. Uphold us during this time of prayer and may our lives reflect your beauty.

Through the ages you have guided us, your pilgrim people; speak to us today and renew the face of the earth: sustain us by your word,
may your birth bring us joy.

You have shown us the ways of peace and reconciliation. Be with those who struggle to have their rights respected: sustain us by your word,
may your birth bring us joy.

You came among us in poverty and were driven into exile. Keep in your special care those who are deprived of home and country: sustain us by your word,
may your birth bring us joy.

Your first home was a stable and your bed a manger. Be with those who have no home and encourage your Church to work for the alleviation of homelessness: sustain us by your word, **may your birth bring us joy.**

Enable us to reach out in love and charity to the world. Bless the efforts of this church ....: sustain us by your word, **may your birth bring us joy.**

Amid the pressures of living in our world today, uphold all families with your love and joy: sustain us by your word, **may your birth bring us joy.**

Epiphany Season

January 6 to February 2

Sundays to Saturdays

Sundays

We come before you, O Lord, with nothing except the gift of our hearts in prayer. Hear us and bring us your peace.

Heal the divisions of your church, so that we may bear witness to your saving love in a broken and divided world. Bless our work for Christian unity in this place ....: Christ, revealed in the flesh,
show us your glory.

Bring peace to our troubled world and sow love in the hearts of all your children: Christ, revealed in the flesh,
show us your glory.

Heal the sick, comfort the afflicted and be with those who mourn the loss of loved ones ....: Christ, revealed in the flesh,
show us your glory.

May your name be proclaimed to all the peoples of the world: Christ, revealed in the flesh,
show us your glory.

Your glory has been shown to the world. Bless us in this parish
..........: Christ, revealed in the flesh,
show us your glory.

Keep in safety those who travel; may they arrive at their journey's end: Christ, revealed in the flesh,
show us your glory.

Mondays

All nations bow down before you, O Lord. Come to us, accept
the homage of our hearts and hear the cries of your people.

Stir in us the desire to strive for unity among all Christians;
pour your blessings upon our partnerships with the churches of
this area ....: Christ, vindicated in the Spirit,
show your love to us this day.

Enable us to work for the peace of the world: Christ, vindicated
in the Spirit,
show your love to us this day.

Enter the lives of all who are sick and in need, that they may
enjoy the touch of your healing love: Christ, vindicated in the
Spirit,
show your love to us this day.

May all peoples come to the knowledge and love of you. Be
with mission agencies who strive to make your love known
throughout the world: Christ, vindicated in the Spirit,
show your love to us this day.

May your love be shown in our care of the schools in this parish
.... Bless all teachers with your heavenly wisdom: Christ,
vindicated in the Spirit,
show your love to us this day.

Keep in your special care all who travel: Christ, vindicated in
the Spirit,
show your love to us this day.

Tuesdays

You will deliver the poor who cry out to you. Listen, Lord, to
the prayers of your people who long for deliverance.

Forgive us, your Church, for the darkness of our disunity.
Direct and guide our efforts and draw us closer to you ....:
Christ, seen by angels,
may we share the joys of heaven.

May the light of peace shine in the hearts of all your children
and may all nations pursue the path of love: Christ, seen by
angels,
may we share the joys of heaven.

Bring healing to those whose lives are scarred by pain and sickness. We pray for local hospitals and surgeries ....; let your
light shine in their hearts and lives: Christ, seen by angels,
may we share the joys of heaven.

Bring all nations and peoples to the light of the gospel: Christ,
seen by angels,
may we share the joys of heaven.

Protect all who travel and keep them in your care: Christ, seen by angels,
may we share the joys of heaven.

Wednesdays

Lord God, you show your pity for the weak and the poor. Hear the humble prayers of your children.

Lord Jesus, stir our hearts and give us the desire to live in unity with all Christians ....: Christ, proclaimed among the nations,
shine in our hearts.

We bring before you, O Lord, countries caught up in war and violence. Graft in our hearts the love of peace: Christ, proclaimed among the nations,
shine in our hearts.

We pray for the sick in body, mind or spirit. Comfort them with the knowledge of your presence: Christ, proclaimed among the nations,
shine in our hearts.

Be with all missionaries, particularly those who work in lonely and isolated places: Christ, proclaimed among the nations,
shine in our hearts.

We pray for all who work in our parish .... Christ, proclaimed among the nations,
shine in our hearts.

Keep safe and be with those who travel: Christ, proclaimed among the nations,
shine in our hearts.

Thursdays

Hear us, Lord, in this time of prayer.

Lord God, deliver us from the prison of our insularity, enlarge our hearts to seek unity with all Christians and bless the partnerships we have forged in this place ....: Christ, believed in throughout the world,
we are your children.

Lord God, bring in your reign of peace, so that all may enjoy the fruits of your love: Christ, believed in throughout the world,
we are your children.

Lord God, heal the sick .... Reveal your kingdom in mighty deeds and awesome signs: Christ, believed in throughout the world,
we are your children.

Lord God, show your love to all people. Let us share in the inheritance that you have promised to those who believe in you: Christ, believed in throughout the world,
we are your children.

Lord God, bless those who work in our local authority. We pray for all who work in our education services ....: Christ, believed in throughout the world,
we are your children.

Lord God, bless those who travel, that they may arrive at their destination in peace, safety and joy: Christ, believed in throughout the world,
we are your children.

Fridays

Hear us, Lord; come near to us and bless us, for we long for the radiant light of your glory.

May your Church on earth reflect the fullness of the unity and joy of heaven; pour down your blessings upon our work ....: Christ, taken up in glory,
light of all light, show us your glory.

Bless all who work for peace and mutual understanding in our world: Christ, taken up in glory,
light of all light, show us your glory.

Comfort the sick, bring them your healing and renew their lives in your service: Christ, taken up in glory,
light of all light, show us your glory.

May your word be sown in the hearts of all peoples, so that your children may be gathered up to you: Christ, taken up in glory,
light of all light, show us your glory.

Shine in the hearts of those who hold authority both nationally and locally ....: Christ, taken up in glory,
light of all light, show us your glory.

Bless those who travel, protect them with your mighty power: Christ, taken up in glory,
light of all light, show us your glory.

Saturdays

Live in our hearts, Lord God, as we pray and give praise to you, the light of the world.

Gather all your children in love. Bless all who work and strive for unity, particularly in this parish ....: Christ, whose will shall be made manifest,
rule in our hearts.

Govern the hearts and minds of your children, particularly those whose hearts are hardened by war and violence. Bend their hearts to your will: Christ, whose will shall be made manifest,
rule in our hearts.

Bring your healing love and power to those who are sick and in need. Bless the work of all who are engaged in caring for the sick: Christ, whose will shall be made manifest,
rule in our hearts.

Gather your children to worship you, so that your will may be completed in us: Christ, whose will shall be made manifest,
rule in our hearts.

Encourage us to look outwards to the world in our service and care .... Be with us lest we labour in vain: Christ, whose will shall be made manifest,
rule in our hearts.

Protect those who travel, guide them in your love and assure them of your compassion: Christ, whose will shall be made manifest,
rule in our hearts.

Lent

Sundays to Saturdays

Sundays

Lord God, in your mercy turn your face from our sins, forgive us and hear the prayers of our hearts.

We bring before you, O Lord, all those who are preparing for baptism and confirmation. May they walk in newness of life: Lord Jesus, you are full of gentleness,
gather your children to you.

We pray for those who serve the Church in positions of leadership and authority .... May they follow the example of our Lord who came among us as servant of all: Lord Jesus, you are full of gentleness,
gather your children to you.

Comfort and lighten the burden of guilt of those who are weighed down by sin. May they seek the newness of life that comes from repentance, contrition and a desire to lead a new life: Lord Jesus, you are full of gentleness,
gather your children to you.

We pray for those whose lives are consumed by the passing fashions of our day. Give them the desire to seek those things of heavenly value: Lord Jesus, you are full of gentleness,
gather your children to you.

Bless our parish during this season of Lent; may it be a time of almsgiving, prayer and study ....: Lord Jesus, you are full of gentleness,
gather your children to you.

We bring before you those who are hungry. Increase our efforts during this season to create a more just world: Lord Jesus, you are full of gentleness,
gather your children to you.

Mondays

You are slow to anger and abound in love; hear our prayers which we bring before you in penitence and faith.

Shower your blessings on those who are preparing for baptism and confirmation, particularly those in this parish ....: Lord Jesus, in your love remake us,
and have mercy on us.

Give our leaders the desire to follow the example of our Lord, who was content to serve his disciples: Lord Jesus, in your love remake us,
and have mercy on us.

You are all tenderness and love. Shower your mercy on those who seek forgiveness: Lord Jesus, in your love remake us,
and have mercy on us.

Bring back and restore those who have wandered from your path. In your mercy and graciousness, bless them: Lord Jesus, in your love remake us,
and have mercy on us.

Bless us in our witness to the schools of this area ....: Lord Jesus, in your love remake us,
and have mercy on us.

Feed the hungry and give us a deep desire to restore your children to fullness of life: Lord Jesus, in your love remake us,
and have mercy on us.

Tuesdays

Hear the prayers of our hearts, Lord God, for we come to you conscious of our own frailties.

Stir in those preparing for baptism and confirmation the will and desire to finish the race that lies before them: may your love prepare us for the joys of heaven,
so that we share eternity with you.

May all who hold authority have before them the example of our Lord's to serve and not to be served: may your love prepare us for the joys of heaven,
so that we share eternity with you.

Bless us during this season of Lent. May we use it as a time of self-reflection so that your forgiveness releases us to serve you better in the world: may your love prepare us for the joys of heaven,
so that we share eternity with you.

Surround with your love all who care for the sick .... Bless doctors and nurses and give them the gifts of patience and love; bless our local hospitals ....: may your love prepare us for the joys of heaven,
so that we share eternity with you.

Forgive us the times when we have exchanged the lasting values of your gospel for the perishable and transitory values of the world: may your love prepare us for the joys of heaven,
so that we share eternity with you.

Pour into our hearts the will to serve you in feeding the hungry. May we use this season as a time of generosity and overflowing love: may your love prepare us for the joys of heaven,
so that we share eternity with you.

Wednesdays

We delight in your law, O God; may the prayers of our hearts reflect your will for us.

Pour your Spirit into the hearts of all those who are being baptized and confirmed. Give them the needful gifts of grace: Lord, may your law give us life,
that we may delight in your will.

May all who serve us through their leadership have before them the perfect law of Christ: Lord, may your law give us life,
that we may delight in your will.

Unburden those who are weighed down by sin and guilt. Restore and forgive those who, in humility, seek reconciliation with you: Lord, may your law give us life,
that we may delight in your will.

Seek out those whose lives have been compromised by the false and shallow values of this world: Lord, may your law give us life,
that we may delight in your will.

Pour your love upon all who work in this parish and bless our places of work ....: Lord, may your law give us life,
that we may delight in your will.

Fill those who are hungry and pour into our hearts a desire for your will to be done on earth as it is in heaven: Lord, may your law give us life,
that we may delight in your will.

Thursdays

Lord God, the poor cry out for justice, the hungry for food and the prisoner for release. Hear our prayers for all your children in their need.

May your ways become rooted in the hearts of all who are being baptized and confirmed: Lord, we cry to you,
hear and answer our prayer.

Bless our leaders. May they promote, through their own example, lives that are filled with the spirit of service: Lord, we cry to you,
hear and answer our prayer.

May all who are burdened by the weight of sin be restored to the fullness of joy, reconciliation and love: Lord, we cry to you,
hear and answer our prayer.

Bring back those who have followed the ways of the world. May this season be a time of restoration for us, when we turn back to you: Lord, we cry to you,
hear and answer our prayer.

Give a spirit of service to those who work for the local authority .... We pray for the emergency services in this locality ....: Lord, we cry to you,
hear and answer our prayer.

Enable our own fasting to loose the bonds of injustice that cause your children to suffer hunger. Create in our hearts a desire for a better world: Lord, we cry to you,
hear and answer our prayer.

Fridays

Lord Jesus, you know the secret thoughts of our hearts. Direct our ways to seek your will; hear the cry of our hearts as we come before you in prayer.

Bless those who are preparing for baptism and confirmation. Sow in their hearts a spirit of prayer and love: Jesus, Saviour of the world,
through your cross you have restored our life.

Pour into the hearts of our leaders the gifts of service and love: Jesus, Saviour of the world,
through your cross you have restored our life.

May all who seek forgiveness come to you, the source of love and reconciliation. Guide us to the foot of the cross: Jesus, Saviour of the world,
through your cross you have restored our life.

Protect the faint-hearted and the wayward; enable them to follow the way of the cross: Jesus, Saviour of the world,
through your cross you have restored our life.

Guide with your love and care our local councillors ....
Instil in them a spirit of dedication and service: Jesus, Saviour of the world,
through your cross you have restored our life.

May this season be for us a time of overflowing love and generosity as we respond in faith to the cries of those who are hungry and poor: Jesus, Saviour of the world,
through your cross you have restored our life.

Saturdays

Enter our hearts, Lord Jesus Christ; may your will be discerned in our prayers and in our lives.

Bless all who are seeking to do your will through the sacrament of baptism. May they respond to your call in faith and love: we glorify you, O Lord,
renew us by your grace.

Enable those who serve you in positions of leadership to sit at your feet and ponder your words of love and service: we glorify you, O Lord,
renew us by your grace.

Bless those who are seeking your forgiveness. May they be gentle on themselves and find in you the source of compassion and love: we glorify you, O Lord,
renew us by your grace.

Forgive, Lord, all those who through thoughtlessness and pride follow the false gods of this age. Restore them to your Church: we glorify you, O Lord,
renew us by your grace.

Stir our hearts to deeds of love; bless this parish in our ministry. We pray in particular for the care we give to the elderly ....: we glorify you, O Lord,
renew us by your grace.

Feed the hungry and enable us to work for the restoration of your justice and peace: we glorify you, O Lord,
renew us by your grace.

Passiontide

The last two weeks of Lent, from the Fifth Sunday of Lent until Easter Eve

Sundays to Saturdays

Sundays

Our trust and our hope lie in you, Lord God; hear our prayers and deliver us.

Be with all Christians who face suffering and persecution for their faith. We give thanks for the witness of their courage: we adore you, O Christ, and we bless you,
because by your holy cross you have redeemed the world.

We pray for all peoples who face oppression and violence. Stir in us, O Lord, the will to work for your justice: we adore you, O Christ, and we bless you,
because by your holy cross you have redeemed the world.

Comfort the lonely; be their strength, their life and their joy: we adore you, O Christ, and we bless you,
because by your holy cross you have redeemed the world.

Tend the dying, and bless those who care for them: we adore you, O Christ, and we bless you,
because by your holy cross you have redeemed the world.

May this Passiontide be for us a time of reflection and prayer. Bless us as we strive to come close to you ....: we adore you, O Christ, and we bless you,
because by your holy cross you have redeemed the world.

Be near to those who are facing the loss of loved ones. Comfort them with your tenderness and compassion: we adore you, O Christ, and we bless you,
because by your holy cross you have redeemed the world.

Mondays

We place our trust in your loving mercy; hear the cry of our hearts, Lord Jesus Christ.

We pray for Christians for whom the cross is a living, daily reality. We pray for .... May they gain strength from your cross: let us set our minds on the things of God,
so that we may grow in love.

Bless all who work for the dignity of human life. May those who face oppression have their rights and dignity respected: let us set our minds on the things of God,
so that we may grow in love.

Be with the lonely and those whose hearts and minds are troubled: let us set our minds on the things of God,
so that we may grow in love.

We pray for the dying, particularly those who face death without the comfort of family and friends: let us set our minds on the things of God,
so that we may grow in love.

We pray for our local schools .... Be with pupils, staff, governors and parents: let us set our minds on the things of God,
so that we may grow in love.

Comfort the bereaved; may they be assured of your love and tenderness: let us set our minds on the things of God,
so that we may grow in love.

Tuesdays

You were crushed for our iniquities and wounded for our transgressions; hear the prayers of those who cry out to you in faith.

Remember, O Lord, those Christians who bear the marks of suffering in their lives. Comfort and strengthen them with your presence: may your wounds heal us,
and bring us to new life.

Remember those who are destroyed by the weight of oppression. Give courage to all who work to relieve suffering: may your wounds heal us,
and bring us to new life.

Hold in your hands the lonely and those whose lives are marred by the absence of family and friends. Assure them of your love and comfort: may your wounds heal us,
and bring us to new life.

Accompany those who are facing death. Be with those who work in our hospices. We pray in particular for our local hospice ....: may your wounds heal us,
and bring us to new life.

Remember those who are crushed by the loss of loved ones. Let them feel the power and tenderness of your all-embracing love: may your wounds heal us,
and bring us to new life.

Wednesdays

We long for your mercy and loving kindness; hear us, O Lord our God.

May we always have before us the needs of our fellow Christians who face persecution. Be their constant companion: we proclaim Christ crucified,
for it is through the cross that we are saved.

We pray for peoples who are weighed down by oppression and violence. We pray for ....: we proclaim Christ crucified,
for it is through the cross that we are saved.

Bring to those who are lonely the comfort and peace of your most sacred heart: we proclaim Christ crucified,
for it is through the cross that we are saved.

Embrace those who are facing death. May their final journey be accompanied not only by friends but by the promise of your eternal peace: we proclaim Christ crucified,
for it is through the cross that we are saved.

Bless all who witness to your universal love in the world of work. Uphold those who help our local economy ....Guide with your love those who cannot work: we proclaim Christ crucified,
for it is through the cross that we are saved.

We pray for all who are facing the loneliness of bereavement. May they be assured of your love and comfort: we proclaim Christ crucified,
for it is through the cross that we are saved.

Thursdays

Confident of your loving mercy and faithfulness, we come to you, O Lord.

We pray for those communities who through their life bear witness to the sufferings of our crucified Lord. We pray for ....
Bring them your peace: Christ the Good Shepherd, guard us,
and lead us to do your will.

Protect all those whose lives are marred by violence and oppression. Assure them of your love and peace: Christ the Good Shepherd, guard us,
and lead us to do your will.

Embrace with your love and tenderness those who are lonely. Enable us to reach out in love and compassion to those who need our help: Christ the Good Shepherd, guard us,
and lead us to do your will.

In the shadow of your wings, comfort those who are facing

death. Be with all who work in our hospices and hospitals bringing comfort and peace: Christ the Good Shepherd, guard us,
and lead us to do your will.

We pray for those who work for our local authority, particularly those entrusted with the care of housing and sheltering the homeless ....: Christ the Good Shepherd, guard us,
and lead us to do your will.

Bless those who are lonely because they mourn the loss of loved ones. Accompany them with the graciousness of your presence: Christ the Good Shepherd, guard us,
and lead us to do your will.

Fridays

Save us, O Lord; hear our prayers, for we long for your loving kindness.

Be with communities who face persecution because of their faith. We pray for .... We give thanks for their witness and courage: Lord, we pray to you with all our heart,
hear us as we cry to you.

We bring before you all who are oppressed and those whose rights are violated and abused ....: Lord, we pray to you with all our heart,
hear us as we cry to you.

Be with the lonely and comfort them with your tender and compassionate love: Lord, we pray to you with all our heart,
hear us as we cry to you.

Be the support and care of those who face death. Comfort and uphold them with the gentle strength of your love: Lord, we pray to you with all our heart,
hear us as we cry to you.

Be with our local politicians .... May they be assured of our prayers: Lord, we pray to you with all our heart,
hear us as we cry to you.

Tend those who face the loss of loved ones. Sanctify the ministry of those who look after and care for the bereaved: Lord, we pray to you with all our heart,
hear us as we cry to you.

Saturdays

Out of the depths of our longings and desires, we come to you, O Lord, to pray for the needs of your children.

You called the persecuted blessed. Enable them to share in the joy of the kingdom of heaven: Jesus, from the wood of the cross you are reigning,
may your death and life reap a harvest of good fruit.

Bless those who live in the shadow of violence and oppression. Turn the hearts of those who perpetrate acts of violence to repentance: Jesus, from the wood of the cross you are reigning,
may your death and life reap a harvest of good fruit.

Be the constant companion of those who are lonely; be their joy and their love: Jesus, from the wood of the cross you are reigning,
may your death and life reap a harvest of good fruit.

Give courage to all who are dying. Be with those who care for them in our hospices, hospitals and nursing homes: Jesus, from the wood of the cross you are reigning,
may your death and life reap a harvest of good fruit.

Bless the work of this parish, particularly our work with young families and children ....: Jesus, from the wood of the cross you are reigning,
may your death and life reap a harvest of good fruit.

Give purpose and strength to those who are facing the loss of loved ones: Jesus, from the wood of the cross you are reigning,
may your death and life reap a harvest of good fruit.

Easter Season

Easter Day to the day before Ascension Day

Sundays to Saturdays

Sundays

Through your resurrection you have given us an inheritance which is imperishable and undefiled. We come to you in joy to give thanks for the new life you have promised us.

We praise you on this great day of joy, for you have brought us to a new and living hope through the resurrection of Jesus Christ from the dead. Bless this parish as we celebrate your resurrection: risen and glorified Lord,
you have given us new birth.

Through your resurrection the whole of creation is renewed. Forgive our lack of vision in caring for the world you created: risen and glorified Lord,
you have given us new birth.

Your new life has brought us out of the darkness of fear and sin. Be with those who have lost hope in the promise of your

resurrection life: risen and glorified Lord,
you have given us new birth.

Bless those whose hope in the resurrection is blighted by the fear of death. May the reality of the empty tomb shatter the bonds of apprehension: risen and glorified Lord,
you have given us new birth.

Be with all prisoners and captives. Let your light shine in their hearts: risen and glorified Lord,
you have given us new birth.

Mondays

Lord God, you are in our midst, and through your resurrection you renew us in your love. Pour your grace upon us during this time of prayer.

Sow in the hearts of Christians the spirit of joy, that we may proclaim the risen Christ: daughter of Jerusalem, sing and shout for joy,
for the Lord has risen. Alleluia.

Bless those who alert us to the needs of your creation. Give us hearts that are enlarged with hope and love for all your creatures: daughter of Jerusalem, sing and shout for joy,
for the Lord has risen. Alleluia.

Be with those who have no faith and those whose faith in God and humanity has been diminished. Instil in your children the light of faith: daughter of Jerusalem, sing and shout for joy,
for the Lord has risen. Alleluia.

May the undimmed glory of the empty tomb shine in the hearts of those who live in the shadow of death. Sow in the hearts of your children the abiding hope of new life: daughter of Jerusalem, sing and shout for joy,
for the Lord has risen. Alleluia.

Bless the witness of this church in the life of our local schools .... Enable us to participate in the activities of our schools, that your love may be revealed in our service: daughter of Jerusalem, sing and shout for joy,
for the Lord has risen. Alleluia.

Bless prisoners and their families. We give thanks for all who work in the probation service and for the rehabilitation of prisoners: daughter of Jerusalem, sing and shout for joy,
for the Lord has risen. Alleluia.

Tuesdays

Through your mighty resurrection we have been offered fullness of life, sown in weakness and raised in power. Confident of your mercies we come to you in prayer.

Enable us to respond with joy to the Good News of the resurrection and proclaim your glory to the ends of the earth: set our hearts on your kingdom, O Lord,
and renew the face of the earth.

The whole of creation is groaning with eager longing for salvation. Inspire our efforts to be responsible stewards of the earth's resources: set our hearts on your kingdom, O Lord,
and renew the face of the earth.

Cover with your wings those who live in the midst of darkness and despair .... Raise them up, O Lord, that they may see the glory of your life: set our hearts on your kingdom, O Lord, **and renew the face of the earth.**

Tend and soothe those who are facing death. May your resurrection be their strength and comfort: set our hearts on your kingdom, O Lord,
and renew the face of the earth.

Bless the work of our hospitals .... We pray for patients, doctors, nurses and all who work to comfort and heal the sick. We pray for any known to us who are sick ....: set our hearts on your kingdom, O Lord,
and renew the face of the earth.

Show your mercy to all prisoners. Bless their families and friends: set our hearts on your kingdom, O Lord,
and renew the face of the earth.

Wednesdays

Set our hearts on things that are above.

In our life and witness, teach us to seek the things that are above. Enable us to preach the Good News of your risen life: ever-living Christ,
hear our prayer.

Help us to witness to your love. May it embrace the needs and demands of being responsible stewards of your creation: ever-living Christ,
hear our prayer.

We pray for those who are caught up in the darkness of despair. Reveal to them the eternal hope that you have promised through your resurrection from the dead: ever-living Christ,
hear our prayer.

We bring before you those who are dying. May they hold fast to the faith: ever-living Christ,
hear our prayer.

Guide and defend those who work in this parish .... We pray for those who are facing unemployment, particularly those who have asked for our prayers ....: ever-living Christ,
hear our prayer.

May we reflect your own compassion in our treatment of those who are prisoners and captives: ever-living Christ,
hear our prayer.

Thursdays

Open our eyes to your presence among us and let this time of prayer be blessed by the radiance of your glory.

Bless us in our journey of faith; enable us to bring others to the new life that you have promised us: Lord, stay with us always,
and be our constant companion.

We give thanks for those whose prophetic example enables us to care for the world; for the endeavours of scientists and campaigners who alert us to the dangers before us: Lord, stay with us always,
and be our constant companion.

Journey with those who live with the darkness of despair: Lord, stay with us always,
and be our constant companion.

Accompany those who are facing death. Lighten their burden and fill them with the hope of the glory that lies before them: Lord, stay with us always,
and be our constant companion.

Bless with your unfailing love those who work for our local authority of N .... We pray for our social services and for local agencies who care for the vulnerable ....: Lord, stay with us always,
and be our constant companion.

We pray for those in prison. Be with them and reveal to them the light of your presence: Lord, stay with us always,
and be our constant companion.

Fridays

We are assured of your resurrection, Lord. In faith and trust we come to you in prayer.

In the joy of this season, give us grace to proclaim your everlasting rule: risen Lord, hear us,
and let our cry come to you.

Give us courage to face the often unpalatable truths of our inaction, indifference and lack of stewardship of the earth's resources: risen Lord, hear us,
and let our cry come to you.

We pray for those in despair. May we embrace your children through our own ministry of care and love: risen Lord, hear us,
and let our cry come to you.

Comfort the dying. Fill them with your love, compassion and the hope of eternal life: risen Lord, hear us,
and let our cry come to you.

Be the strength and support of our local councillors ....
Give them the spirit of joy that comes from true service: risen Lord, hear us,
and let our cry come to you.

Be near to those who are imprisoned. Show them the love that releases us from the bonds of selfishness and despair: risen Lord, hear us,
and let our cry come to you.

Saturdays

Lord Jesus, you are the first and the last and you are alive for ever. Come to our hearts as we make our prayer to you.

Through your resurrection you have filled us with new hope and new life. Give us grace to proclaim your glory; bless this parish in our witness to the life-giving love of Jesus ....:
Lord Jesus, bless us your children,
and fill us with your love.

Bless those whose efforts to create a lasting stewardship of the earth's resources have resulted in responsible living. Create in

our own hearts that desire to care for the earth: Lord Jesus,
bless us your children,
and fill us with your love.

Comfort those who live with depression and despair. May they
find their hope and rest in the risen Lord: Lord Jesus, bless us
your children,
and fill us with your love.

We pray for the dying, that their fear may be calmed by the
comfort of friends and family, and through faith in your eternal
promises: Lord Jesus, bless us your children,
and fill us with your love.

Be with prisoners. Comfort them with the assurance of your
presence and love: Lord Jesus, bless us your children,
and fill us with your love.

Ascension Day to Pentecost

Ascension Day

Lord Jesus, you have ascended to your father. Hear the prayers we bring before you.

On this day you ascended on high to reign for ever as Lord and King. May we acknowledge your kingly and priestly rule and so come to share in this inheritance: mighty Lord, you have ascended in triumph,
may we share your glory.

On this day we pray for the gifts of patience and fortitude. Help us to wait in faith and grow in holiness: mighty Lord, you have ascended in triumph,
may we share your glory.

On this day your earthly victory was sealed by your ascension. Show this triumph to the peoples of the earth, that we may acknowledge your just rule: mighty Lord, you have ascended in triumph,
may we share your glory.

On this day you promised to be with us until the end of time. Enable us to work responsibly and carefully for the earth, for all our futures and for the good of everyone: mighty Lord, you have ascended in triumph,
may we share your glory.

On this day you have shown your power and might to the nations. Bless those who exercise their authority in our community. In particular, we pray for our local council ....: mighty Lord, you have ascended in triumph,
may we share your glory.

On this day you ascended on high to be with your Father. Bless those whose relationships are broken and in need of your healing: mighty Lord, you have ascended in triumph,
may we share your glory.

Friday after Ascension Day

You have promised us a share in your glory. Be with us at this time of prayer as we plead before you.

Jesus, now crowned with glory and splendour, send us the Holy Spirit and reveal your glory in the world: to Christ be praise and glory,
he is worthy to be praised and exalted for ever.

Jesus, the pioneer of our salvation, we wait in hope for the renewal of the earth: to Christ be praise and glory,
he is worthy to be praised and exalted for ever.

Jesus, king of all, enable your children to be subject to your just and gentle rule. We pray for our local mayor and our MP .... May your reign of gentleness and love be the model for all authority: to Christ be praise and glory,
he is worthy to be praised and exalted for ever.

Jesus, reigning on high, you crown the year with your goodness. Pour your blessings on the earth. Give us rich and fruitful harvests, for our bounty is but a reflection of your great providence: to Christ be praise and glory,
he is worthy to be praised and exalted for ever.

Jesus, source of unity and love, bless those who have troubled relationships: to Christ be praise and glory,
he is worthy to be praised and exalted for ever.

Saturday after Ascension Day

Nothing, O Lord, can separate us from your tender love. Be with us during this time of intercession.

Establish your peace in our hearts. We pray for the doubting; enter their lives with your gracious presence: nothing can separate us from you, O Lord,
for your love conquers all things.

Renew your faithful people, so that we may acknowledge your majesty and love for us: nothing can separate us from you, O Lord,
for your love conquers all things.

Your heavenly kingdom will last for ever. May your children acknowledge your saving love: nothing can separate us from you, O Lord,
for your love conquers all things.

Inspire our stewardship of the earth's resources. May our harvests be plentiful and may we give generously of the fruits of the earth: nothing can separate us from you, O Lord,
for your love conquers all things.

Bless this parish in our ministry .... May we witness to your heavenly rule with gentleness and compassion: nothing can separate us from you, O Lord,
for your love conquers all things.

May your love transform the relationships of those who experience heartbreak: nothing can separate us from you, O Lord, **for your love conquers all things.**

Sunday after Ascension Day

We thirst for your love, O Lord. Enter into our hearts during this time of prayer and encourage us with your constant presence.

Pour your Spirit into the Church, that she may proclaim your lordship to the whole world. We ask for your blessings upon this parish ....: like a weary land our soul thirsts for you, **give us your living water always.**

May all who come to you, the well of life and the eternal spring, quench their longing: like a weary land our soul thirsts for you,
give us your living water always.

Bless all who come to you in faith and love. May your kingdom be established in the hearts of your children: like a weary land our soul thirsts for you,
give us your living water always.

Bless those who work on the land. We rejoice in your constant bounty: like a weary land our soul thirsts for you,
give us your living water always.

Come Holy Spirit and pour out your reconciling love on those relationships blighted by quarrels and indifference: like a weary land our soul thirsts for you,
give us your living water always.

Monday after Ascension Day

You give power to the faint and strength to the weak. Uphold us during this time of prayer.

You, Lord God, rule over us in power and might. Give your Church grace and courage to proclaim your kingdom and to live according to your will: we wait for you, O Lord,
pour your strength into our hearts.

We pray for those who are anxious and troubled. May they find in you the source of all life and power: we wait for you, O Lord,
pour your strength into our hearts.

May your kingly power establish itself in the hearts of your people: we wait for you, O Lord,
pour your strength into our hearts.

Bless the earth and our stewardship of it. May we sow and reap bountifully so that your kingly rule may be established: we wait for you, O Lord,
pour your strength into our hearts.

Christ the teacher, pour your love into our schools. We pray particularly for the schools in this area ....: we wait for you, O Lord,
pour your strength into our hearts.

Rekindle love in relationships that are broken and damaged. May your love reign in us: we wait for you, O Lord,
pour your strength into our hearts.

Tuesday after Ascension Day

We wait for your loving kindness, O Lord. Enter our hearts and kindle in them the fire of your love.

You have given us the spirit of service. Enable us to fulfil your will and to empower your children to serve you in serving one another: pour your Spirit upon the Church,
so that we may faithfully serve you.

Renew your Church in the power of the Holy Spirit. May we use these days fruitfully in prayer, study and worship: pour your Spirit upon the Church,
so that we may faithfully serve you.

Establish your kingdom in the hearts and minds of those who do not yet know and love you: pour your Spirit upon the Church,
so that we may faithfully serve you.

We pray for productive and fruitful harvests. Bless with your loving kindness all who work on the land: pour your Spirit upon the Church,
so that we may faithfully serve you.

Bless the Church's witness in our hospitals, in particular our local hospital .... We pray for hospital chaplains as they witness to your saving love, and for those who are sick .... Comfort them with the assurance of your presence: pour your Spirit upon the Church,
so that we may faithfully serve you.

Pour your healing balm on those whose relationships are at breaking point. We pray for those who struggle to communicate their anxieties and those who live with depression: pour your Spirit upon the Church,
so that we may faithfully serve you.

Wednesday after Ascension Day

Fill our hearts with the gift of your Spirit, O Lord. Bless this time of prayer.

Through your glorious ascension we see your power and majesty. Teach us how to worship you in spirit and in truth: pour your Spirit on us,
so that we may see your will.

Give us the gifts of faith and peace. May we find renewal and joy in believing: pour your Spirit on us,
so that we may see your will.

You rule with love over the whole of creation. May all people acknowledge your kingdom: pour your Spirit on us,
so that we may see your will.

We remember those who work on the land. Give us a rich harvest and the will to share generously: pour your Spirit on us,
so that we may see your will.

Bless those who hold executive authority in the workplace; guide them in the responsibilities they face. We pray for local companies and for all who are employed by them ....: pour your Spirit on us,
so that we may see your will.

We pray for those whose lives are scarred by broken relation-ships. Shed your love upon them: pour your Spirit on us,
so that we may see your will.

Thursday after Ascension Day

We come as children to you, O Lord, confident that you hear our every need.

You have ascended on high and reign for ever as the High Priest of the new and everlasting covenant. May your love transform us: bless us, your children,
and send us your Spirit.

Bless us in our pilgrimage of life. Guide our efforts and renew our strength: bless us, your children,
and send us your Spirit.

Your rule is over all your works and your righteousness extends throughout the world. May all peoples come to acknowledge your lordship: bless us, your children,
and send us your Spirit.

Bless the earth and our stewardship of it. May the earth yield its fruit in due season so that we may witness your generous love: bless us, your children,
and send us your Spirit.

Bless our local community. We pray for those who work with prisoners, particularly our local probation service ....:
bless us, your children,
and send us your Spirit.

Comfort and support those whose relationships are broken.
Guide with your infinite love those who need our prayers: bless
us, your children,
and send us your Spirit.

Friday after Ascension Day

You have anointed us through the outpouring of your Holy
Spirit. Enliven this time of prayer so that your love may shine
in our hearts.

Through your holy ascension you have promised to be with us
to the end of time. Establish your rule in our lives by sending us
the Holy Spirit: your promises have been given to us,
in faith and hope we say 'Amen'.

We wait to be made holy. Bless us and keep us always under
the shadow of your protecting wings: your promises have been
given to us,
in faith and hope we say 'Amen'.

Your just and kingly rule is over all. May the world sing your
praises and acknowledge your might: your promises have been
given to us,
in faith and hope we say 'Amen'.

We give thanks for the fruits of the earth, for the skill and
dedication of all who work on the land. May the earth produce
bountiful harvests: your promises have been given to us,
in faith and hope we say 'Amen'.

Enfold in your love and care all who hold authority in our local
community. We pray for our local councillors .... and for

our MP ....: your promises have been given to us,
in faith and hope we say 'Amen'.

Embrace with your tender love all those who struggle with the breakdown of relationships: your promises have been given to us,
in faith and hope we say 'Amen'.

Saturday after Ascension Day

Your Spirit brings us life. Transform our hearts so that our prayers may be faithful to your will.

Grant us eyes to see your vision for our world today. Give grace to us in this parish; bless our work with the nurture and faith development of adults: transform us, O Lord, through the power of your Spirit,
that we may proclaim the beauty of your truth.

Your Church eagerly awaits the gifts of the Holy Spirit. Come upon us and renew us: transform us, O Lord, through the power of your Spirit,
that we may proclaim the beauty of your truth.

Govern the hearts and minds of your children. May your compassionate and gentle rule establish itself throughout the world: transform us, O Lord, through the power of your Spirit,
that we may proclaim the beauty of your truth.

We give thanks for the earth you have given us. Bless the earth with your abundant goodness; may we reap rich harvests for the benefit of all your children: transform us, O Lord, through the power of your Spirit,
that we may proclaim the beauty of your truth.

Renew and refresh all those who struggle with their relationships. Sow in their hearts a spirit of forgiveness and reconciliation: transform us, O Lord, through the power of your Spirit, **that we may proclaim the beauty of your truth.**

The Day of Pentecost

Pour your Holy Spirit into our hearts, O Lord, that this time of prayer may be sanctified.

We praise you and thank you for the great gift of the Holy Spirit. Come upon us, O Lord, and set us ablaze with love for you: send us your Spirit, O Lord,
and renew the face of the earth.

Come down upon us and fill us with your heavenly grace. Pour down your blessings upon this Church and community ....
Renew and transform our mission and enable us to serve you in the world: send us your Spirit, O Lord,
and renew the face of the earth.

Establish in the hearts of all people your kingdom of justice and peace: send us your Spirit, O Lord,
and renew the face of the earth.

Bless the earth; may it produce fruits and crops of every kind to nourish all your people: send us your Spirit, O Lord,
and renew the face of the earth.

Transform relationships with your grace and love. We remember in particular those who struggle through broken relationships: send us your Spirit, O Lord,
and renew the face of the earth.

Ordinary Time

Between Pentecost and the Eve of Advent

Set 1 Sundays to Saturdays

Sundays

The love of your law is good and holy. Teach us your will and may this time of prayer be sanctified.

Pour your Holy Spirit upon the Church. Lead us into the light of truth, guard us from the darkness of error and direct us in the paths of your law. Give grace to your children in this parish ....: blessed are you, O Lord,
teach us your ways.

Bless our bishops, especially *N* our bishop. May they be faithful shepherds, holy priests and wise administrators: blessed are you, O Lord,
teach us your ways.

May those who hold authority be governed by your rule of justice and mercy: blessed are you, O Lord,
teach us your ways.

You created the world from the formless void and made it good. May we strive to exercise responsible stewardship of the earth's resources: blessed are you, O Lord,
teach us your ways.

Give us grace to respond to our neighbours in their need. Enable us to reach out in love and compassion to the world: blessed are you, O Lord,
teach us your ways.

Mondays

In your mercy, hear the cry of our hearts. May this time of prayer sow the seeds for a harvest of good works.

Lord our God, you have created us for good. Enable all who work in the fields of media, communications and the arts to spread your message of hope and love: open our eyes, O Lord,
that we may see the wonders of your law.

We pray for all who work in the farming industry and fishing industries. Help us to be thankful for all the labours that go to provide food for our tables: open our eyes, O Lord,
that we may see the wonders of your law.

Bless those who work in commerce and industry. Sustain and uphold their work with vision and true hope: open our eyes, O Lord,
that we may see the wonders of your law.

Bless those whose work is unrewarding, those whose lives are characterized by stress and those who live and work with con-

stant danger. Protect them and enfold them with love: open our eyes, O Lord,
that we may see the wonders of your law.

We pray for the schools in this parish .... Bless children, parents and all others entrusted with their care and protection: open our eyes, O Lord,
that we may see the wonders of your law.

Comfort with your love and protection those who are unemployed. Give them a sense of value and self-worth and bring them into the joy of sharing their gifts with others: open our eyes, O Lord,
that we may see the wonders of your law.

Tuesdays

Teach us the ways of your law, that we may hold them dear to our hearts. Bless this time and may your continuing presence crown our lives.

At this hour we pause and remember those who are sick .... Comfort and relieve them: teach us, O Lord, the way of your laws,
and we shall keep them to the end.

Bless all relief workers in areas of famine and other disasters .... May our hearts overflow with compassion that we reach out with loving arms to the suffering of this world: teach us, O Lord, the way of your laws,
and we shall keep them to the end.

Bring comfort to those whose lives are scarred by abuse and violence. Help us to work for the alleviation of such suffering and so hasten the time when your peace reigns in the hearts of your people: teach us, O Lord, the way of your laws,
and we shall keep them to the end.

Comfort the bereaved and bring them your peace: teach us, O Lord, the way of your laws,
and we shall keep them to the end.

We give thanks for doctors, nurses and hospital chaplains. We pray for our local hospital and surgery .... Enable us to value their skill and dedication: teach us, O Lord, the way of your laws,
and we shall keep them to the end.

Wednesdays

Your paths are blessed, your law is good. Direct our hearts in your way and bless this time of prayer.

We pray for those who work in the social services department of our local authority. Give them wisdom and skill in all they undertake: you, O Lord, are gracious and good,
teach us your ways.

Give patient understanding to those who work in our criminal justice system. We pray for the police service, praying in particular for our local police station ...., for those who work in our prisons, for prison wardens, chaplains and those who work for the probation service: you, O Lord, are gracious and good,
teach us your ways.

Tend and comfort those who are the victims of crime and reform the perpetrators. Give us a new vision of a society that is at ease with itself: you, O Lord, are gracious and good,
teach us your ways.

We give thanks for the work of all aid agencies. Strengthen our efforts to create a more just world: you, O Lord, are gracious and good,
teach us your ways.

May your love be the inspiration for all who are employers in this parish; in particular we pray for all shops and retail outlets ....: you, O Lord, are gracious and good,
teach us your ways.

Be the constant guide and comfort of those whose lives are scarred by poverty, deprivation and injustice: you, O Lord, are gracious and good,
teach us your ways.

Thursdays

From everlasting to everlasting you are God; in your mercy and love hear our prayer for all whom we bring before you.

Give grace to all who serve our community in local government. Guide them to serve the needs of all people: O Lord, your word is everlasting,
your law stands firm in the heavens.

We give thanks for those who serve our community in the provision of local services and amenities. We pray for our local libraries and for those who work in them .... Give us grateful hearts: O Lord, your word is everlasting,
your law stands firm in the heavens.

We pray for those who give their lives in caring for others. Teach us truly to value their work: O Lord, your word is everlasting,
your law stands firm in the heavens.

Bless our schools, colleges and universities. Give vision to all who teach and diligence to all who learn: O Lord, your word is everlasting,
your law stands firm in the heavens.

We pray for those who work in our emergency services. Give them a spirit of dedication in their work and courage in all that they undertake on our behalf: O Lord, your word is everlasting,
your law stands firm in the heavens.

Fridays

Your law is a light upon our pilgrim path. Shine in our hearts during this time of prayer; enliven and enlighten our witness.

We offer our thanks for all who serve in the government of this country, for Her Majesty the Queen and the High Court of Parliament. We pray for our armed forces, giving thanks for their skill and dedication. Enable us to seek and work for the common good: your word is a lantern for our feet,
and a light upon our path.

Herald your reign of peace and justice and give courage to all people who work for the needs of your children: your word is a lantern for our feet,
and a light upon our path.

Enfold in your love those who work to bring reconciliation to individuals and communities ....: your word is a lantern for our feet,
and a light upon our path.

May the light of your peace shine in those places in our world that have been devastated by the darkness of war: your word is a lantern for our feet,
and a light upon our path.

Bless those who are in prison; comfort those who are refugees, and may your compassion enfold those who are homeless. Bless our efforts to create a more just and caring society: your word is a lantern for our feet,
and a light upon our path.

Saturdays

Uphold and support us during this time of prayer. Hear the cries of your children who long for salvation.

We give thanks to you, O Lord, for our homes and families and for the joy and company of friends: O Lord, support and hold us,
and we shall be saved.

Bless those who care for others and give their time and energy to nursing sick relatives. Be their support and enable us to value their work: O Lord, support and hold us,
and we shall be saved.

Comfort those who are near the end of their life. Be especially close to those who will be facing death alone: O Lord, support and hold us,
and we shall be saved.

To those who have lost hope, may the light of faith and hope shine in their hearts: O Lord, support and hold us,
and we shall be saved.

Bless the mission of this place, guide us in our work, particularly with children and young adults ....: O Lord, support and hold us,
and we shall be saved.

Bless the worship of this place. Inspire us with your truth and nourish us with your word and sacrament: O Lord, support and hold us,
and we shall be saved.

Set 2 Sundays to Saturdays

Sundays

Lord God, enter our hearts that we may delight in the wonders of your law.

Guide and lead your Church into all truth. Bless us in our outreach and evangelism; in particular we pray for .... May

your gospel be proclaimed to all nations: your wisdom delights our hearts,
we rejoice in your ways.

Bless all who lead our Church. We pray for N our bishop and those who serve on General Synod: your wisdom delights our hearts,
we rejoice in your ways.

May your will be made perfect in the decisions of all who lead our nations. Give them strength and insight in their deliberations: your wisdom delights our hearts,
we rejoice in your ways.

Give courage to those who challenge our complacency over the misuse of the world's resources. May their voices be heard: your wisdom delights our hearts,
we rejoice in your ways.

Be with all who need our prayers today. O Holy Spirit, bring comfort to all who cry to you for help: your wisdom delights our hearts,
we rejoice in your ways.

Mondays

We lay the burdens of our cares and concerns at your feet, for you alone can bear them. Hear us, O Lord our God.

We give thanks for the creativity of artists. May their work inspire us with true hope and vision: give us your rest and peace,
carry the burdens of our hearts.

We pray for those who work in the farming and fishing industries. Enable us to value their work in creating a sustainable environment: give us your rest and peace,
carry the burdens of our hearts.

Give courage and wisdom to all leaders of industry. May they work for the good of all: give us your rest and peace,
carry the burdens of our hearts.

Hold in the hollow of your hand those whose work is hard and unrewarding. Bless those who suffer from stress and fatigue: give us your rest and peace,
carry the burdens of our hearts.

Pour your love into our local schools .... Enable us to witness to your love in them: give us your rest and peace,
carry the burdens of our hearts.

Bring comfort and strength to those who are unemployed. Instil in us a desire to see your face in all your children: give us your rest and peace,
carry the burdens of our hearts.

Tuesdays

In your love and mercy, hear our prayers.

Heal the sick .... Bring your love to all who call to you for help: come to us, O Lord,
bring us your healing.

Be with those who face famine and disaster. Move our hearts and wills to serve you in serving others: come to us, O Lord,
bring us your healing.

Bless those who are persecuted, those who feel vulnerable and afraid. Comfort all whose lives are marred by prejudice and intolerance: come to us, O Lord,
bring us your healing.

Comfort those who are facing the loss of loved ones. May they know your peace and love: come to us, O Lord,
bring us your healing.

Give your strength to those who work in the medical and healing professions. We bring before you the needs of our local hospital .... Teach us to be thankful for the ministry given by hospitals: come to us, O Lord,
bring us your healing.

Wednesdays

Enter our hearts during this time of prayer; scatter all that is selfish and unwise and enable us to listen to the longings of your heart.

Pour your blessing on all who work in the social services. Create in our society that sense of worth of every human being that enables us to value their contribution: fill us with your wisdom,
may your glory cover the earth.

Bless those who work for the administration of justice and the care of prisoners. May your justice permeate our values: fill us with your wisdom,
may your glory cover the earth.

Comfort all victims of crime and those whose acts have made the lives of others intolerable. Teach us to value your children: fill us with your wisdom,
may your glory cover the earth.

Give strength to all who work for the relief of victims of famine and natural disaster. Enable us to respond with open and generous hearts: fill us with your wisdom,
may your glory cover the earth.

Bless those who work in our local area. We pray for the local board of commerce and for all who encourage local business ....: fill us with your wisdom,
may your glory cover the earth.

Help us to show your love to those who live in poverty and those who bear the marks of suffering, oppression and violence. Comfort them at this time of need: fill us with your wisdom,
may your glory cover the earth.

Thursdays

We come to you, confident in your love and mercy, that you hear our every need and that your love surpasses all things.

Give your wisdom and grace to all who serve in local government. May they work for the good of all your children: enable us to serve you,
sow the seed of unity in our hearts.

Bless all who work in providing local services for us. We pray for those who work in the local environmental services ....
May we not take their gifts for granted: enable us to serve you,
sow the seed of unity in our hearts.

Give patient understanding to those who work to make the lives of the young and elderly meaningful .... Make us aware of the needs of all members of our society: enable us to serve you,
sow the seed of unity in our hearts.

Bless those who work in our schools, colleges and universities. Teach us to value their contribution in building a united society where gifts are recognized and built upon ....: enable us to serve you,
sow the seed of unity in our hearts.

We offer thanks and praise for all who put their own lives at risk to help others. Bless them in their work: enable us to serve you,
sow the seed of unity in our hearts.

Fridays

Your kingdom come, O Lord. May this time of prayer bear witness to your authority.

Guide those who hold authority in our land. Bless Her Majesty the Queen, the High Court of Parliament, and all who serve in the armed forces: Lord, teach us to love,
enable us to care for your children.

May your kingdom of love hold sway in the world. Guide us to follow your ways of peace and justice: Lord, teach us to love,
enable us to care for your children.

Bless those who work for peace and reconciliation in communities around the world: Lord, teach us to love,
enable us to care for your children.

Comfort those whose lives are devastated by war and strife. Pour your healing balm into their hearts: Lord, teach us to love,
enable us to care for your children.

Bless our local councillors .... Fill them with wisdom and sow in them the spirit of service: Lord, teach us to love,
enable us to care for your children.

May your peace rest upon those who are prisoners, refugees and homeless. Give us grace and wisdom to see your face in all people: Lord, teach us to love,
enable us to care for your children.

Saturdays

May this time of prayer kindle in us the light of hope and joy.

Bless our homes, families and friends. Enable us to work through difficulties with the spirit of patience and love: open our eyes, O Lord,
that we may see your glory.

Be the comfort and peace of all who care for others. Bless and guide them as they reflect in their lives your compassion and love: open our eyes, O Lord,
that we may see your glory.

Accompany those who are near to death. May they feel the power of your presence and the prayers of those who love them: open our eyes, O Lord,
that we may see your glory.

Bless those whose lives are characterized by depression and despair. Kindle the light of hope in their hearts: open our eyes, O Lord,
that we may see your glory.

Bless our church in our witness to the world .... Enable us to reach out in love and charity so that your children may be free: open our eyes, O Lord,
that we may see your glory.

When two or three are gathered in your name, you are in our midst. Bless our worship and inflame us with the Holy Spirit: open our eyes, O Lord,
that we may see your glory.

Common of Saints

The Blessed Virgin Mary

On this day we give thanks, O God, for the faithful witness of the Blessed Virgin Mary. We come to you conscious of our need to hear your call to us.

The Blessed Virgin Mary, with great humility, listened patiently to your bidding. Give us faithful hearts that we may fulfil your will in our lives: Lord, speak to us,
make us hear your call.

The Blessed Virgin Mary, at the wedding feast in Cana, bid the servants 'Do whatever he tells you'. Teach us, heavenly Father, to be obedient to your will: Lord, speak to us,
make us hear your call.

The Blessed Virgin Mary brought up the child Jesus within the care of a loving family. Bless the families of this church, guide with your especial care our children and our ministry with them .... Lord, speak to us,
make us hear your call.

The Blessed Virgin Mary, her heart torn by grief and sorrow, stood at the foot of the cross. Bless those who are sick .... and those who care for them .... Be with all who minister

to those in need: Lord, speak to us,
make us hear your call.

May the Blessed Virgin Mary, crowned with joy and robed
with the sun, bring all the faithful departed to share in the joys
of heaven. We remember ....: Lord, speak to us,
make us hear your call.

Apostles and Evangelists

Encouraged and supported by the glorious company of apostles and evangelists, we make our prayer to you.

Lord Jesus, you taught your faithful disciples to carry their cross
and follow you daily. Bless us in our daily witness, that your
saving love may be made known: tell of the glory of the Lord,
announce it among the nations.

Lord Jesus, you love the world you made, and sent your apostles
to show that love. Forgive us our self-preoccupations and our
neglect of the world; open our eyes to see a world redeemed:
tell of the glory of the Lord,
announce it among the nations.

Lord Jesus, you formed around you a band of friends who were
faithful and obedient. Bless and guide your Church into the
way of all truth: tell of the glory of the Lord,
announce it among the nations.

Lord Jesus, you bid the disciples to heal the sick. Bless those
entrusted with the care of the sick and dying ....: tell of the
glory of the Lord,
announce it among the nations.

Lord Jesus, you promised the rewards of heaven to your faithful disciples. Bring into your greater presence those who have died ....: tell of the glory of the Lord,
announce it among the nations.

Martyrs

The white-robed army of martyrs praise you, O Lord. We join with them in this time of prayer.

The holy martyrs followed your example of loving to the end. Give your Church the needful gifts of faithful endurance that she may be a witness to your love: let the just sing for joy,
and the upright sing praise.

We pray for Christians who face persecution .... May your love and the example of Saint N *(and N)*, your holy martyr(s), shine in their hearts: let the just sing for joy,
and the upright sing praise.

Bless this parish in our witness to your sacrificial love .... Teach us to love the world that you have made: let the just sing for joy,
and the upright sing praise.

You gave the gift of great faith to your holy martyrs. Bless the sick who long for healing ....: let the just sing for joy,
and the upright sing praise.

You promise the gift of heaven to all your faithful servants. Bless those who have died in the faith .... Grant us with them a share in your eternal victory: let the just sing for joy,
and the upright sing praise.

Teachers of the Faith

Through wise and faithful teachers we have fathomed the depths and climbed the heights of your love. In this time of prayer we join with them in declaring your love for the world.

Through the teaching of your servant *N* we have found the way of faithfulness and discipleship. Give your Church an eagerness to proclaim your love to the world: they will shine brightly in heaven,
they will shine like stars for ever.

Bless those who communicate the truths of the faith through the written word. Be with all writers, composers and artists. Give them the grace to speak of your wisdom to the world: they will shine brightly in heaven,
they will shine like stars for ever.

Bless the work of nurture and education in this parish ....
In a complex and confusing world give us the courage to inspire the faith: they will shine brightly in heaven,
they will shine like stars for ever.

Through your holy word the sick were healed. Bless your Church's ministry in hospitals and hospices .... May your holy words of wisdom bring light and peace to all who are sick: they will shine brightly in heaven,
they will shine like stars for ever.

Bring the faithful departed into the greater glory of your presence, for they were faithful to your word and practised it with great wisdom ....: they will shine brightly in heaven,
they will shine like stars for ever.

Pastors

You have shown your love and gentleness through the ministry of wise and holy pastors. On this day we give thanks for *N*. May we join with *him/her* in the chorus of unending praise as we make our prayers to our heavenly Father.

Bless all priests and deacons; guide them as they seek to make your will known in the ministry of your Church: Christ the Good Shepherd,
feed us, your faithful people.

Through the power of the Holy Spirit guide those who are entrusted with the ministry of preaching and teaching. Fill them with wisdom, that they may break your holy word with care and devotion: Christ the Good Shepherd,
feed us, your faithful people.

In your holy pastor *N* you have taught us that the small seed will reap a great harvest. Be with us in this place and give us the confidence to be dedicated in our ministry ....: Christ the Good Shepherd,
feed us, your faithful people.

Through your holy word you have revealed that the very least belong in the kingdom, and have shown us, through the ministry of your pastors, to care for the sick. Bless the sick .... and bless those who care for them: Christ the Good Shepherd,
feed us, your faithful people.

Be with those who minister to the dying. Give them a heart that speaks of your gentleness and love: Christ the Good Shepherd,
feed us, your faithful people.

Religious

We give thanks for N, whose witness we celebrate today. Enable us, through the working of the Spirit, to grasp hold of the things that really matter in our lives.

You entered the desert and had nowhere to lay your head. We give thanks to God for Saint N and all who have renounced the pleasures of this world to follow you. Give us grace to seek your will wholeheartedly: they left all things and followed Christ,
they have gained eternal life.

You taught us to seek your kingdom. Enable us to walk in your ways after the example of Saint N your faithful servant: they left all things and followed Christ,
they have gained eternal life.

You have taught us to worship you in spirit and in truth. We give thanks for the witness of our religious communities who teach us to seek your will in singleness of heart and devotion to worship, study and prayer: they left all things and followed Christ,
they have gained eternal life.

You taught us that your will lies in service. Bless those orders that serve you in serving the needs of the sick ....: they left all things and followed Christ,
they have gained eternal life.

You have taught us that we live in exile on earth and that our true homeland lies with you in heaven. Bless those who have served you on earth and now worship you in heaven ....: they left all things and followed Christ,
they have gained eternal life.

Missionaries

Through the power of the Holy Spirit we come to God in prayer. Today we give thanks for Saint N who followed the command of God to go out into the world and to preach the kingdom.

Give your Church the power to preach your word to the nations. Bless those in partnership with us in this parish .... Give us gentleness and discernment in our witness, that we may reach out with sensitivity and love: they proclaimed the wonders of God, **all peoples saw his glory.**

Bless the work of this parish and our outreach .... Enable us to preach the gospel with love and care to an anxious and confused world: they proclaimed the wonders of God, **all peoples saw his glory.**

Bless all mission partners throughout the world. We give thanks to God for their witness, praying especially for mission agencies we support through our giving and our prayer .... We pray for those who work in lonely, dangerous and isolated places: they proclaimed the wonders of God, **all peoples saw his glory.**

We pray for those who work in interfaith dialogue, especially .... Pour upon them the gifts of generosity, faithfulness and discernment. May they listen and speak with charity and love: they proclaimed the wonders of God, **all peoples saw his glory.**

We give thanks for all who minister to the sick .... Bless them in their work and make us ever mindful of the needs of those who suffer ....: they proclaimed the wonders of God, **all peoples saw his glory.**

You are with us to the end of the age, and you send us to proclaim this message. Be with those who enjoy your friendship
for ever by your side ....: they proclaimed the wonders of
God,
all peoples saw his glory.

Holy Men and Women

Let us offer our prayers to the throne of the heavenly grace as
we celebrate the witness of your servant(s) Saint *N (and N)*.

Your saints have given us an example of faithfulness to your
word. Enable us to preach and live the message of the gospel in our daily lives: let the hearts that seek you, O Lord,
rejoice,
let them glory in your name.

Your saints have shown us an example of courage and fortitude. Give us the gifts of devotion and constancy, that we may
be faithful to the teaching of the gospel: let the hearts that seek
you, O Lord, rejoice,
let them glory in your name.

Your saints have taught us, through their prayers and writings,
of the things that belong to your will. Enable us to strive for
perfection: let the hearts that seek you, O Lord, rejoice,
let them glory in your name.

Your saints have taught us to care for the sick with constant
love. We pray for those who are in need at this time ....
Enable us to minister to them: let the hearts that seek you, O
Lord, rejoice,
let them glory in your name.

Your saints have pointed us to heaven through the faithfulness
of their lives. We give thanks to you for the faithful departed
.... May they enjoy for ever the peace of your presence: let
the hearts that seek you, O Lord, rejoice,
let them glory in your name.

Special Occasions

The Guidance of the Holy Spirit

We ask you, O Lord, to fill our hearts with your Holy Spirit, that we may give ourselves in love and service.

Inspire your Church, O Lord, with the spirit of love and joy. Fill her with the desire for unity, that we may all be one in you: send us your Holy Spirit, O Lord,
renew us in your service.

Look upon our distracted world, O Lord. Give wisdom and the spirit of peace to all whose hearts are hardened by war and hatred .... send us your Holy Spirit, O Lord,
renew us in your service.

Bless our work and service in this parish .... Instil in our hearts the spirit of patience and understanding: send us your Holy Spirit, O Lord,
renew us in your service.

Guide and inspire all who exercise pastoral ministry in your Church. Bless *N* our bishop. Pour upon all of us the spirit of kindness and faithfulness: send us your Holy Spirit, O Lord,
renew us in your service.

Direct us in the ways of your commandments. Enable us to make a difference to the world we live in through the spirit of gentleness and self-control: send us your Holy Spirit, O Lord,
renew us in your service.

Harvest

We give thanks to God for the bounty of the harvest, for the beauty of the earth and the joy of the seasons that enable us to flourish and grow.

Pour down your blessings upon the Church in her mission, for the fields are ripe for harvest ....: Lord of the harvest,
send down your generous bounty.

We give thanks for those who are involved in the production of our food, for those who work on the land and those who trawl our seas. Help us to be wise in our management of the earth's resources: Lord of the harvest,
send down your generous bounty.

We thank you for those who prepare our food and those whose gift of hospitality enables us to enjoy the fruits of the earth. Pour your blessing on all who provide food and clothing to those in need ....: Lord of the harvest,
send down your generous bounty.

We pray for countries affected by famine .... Help us to reach out in love and charity to those who do not share the joys of the harvest .... and to those whose harvests have failed ....: Lord of the harvest,
send down your generous bounty.

Bring the departed to that eternal banquet in heaven where they will feast for ever in your presence ....: Lord of the harvest, **send down your generous bounty.**

Creation

Creator God, you have given us such beauty in the world. We come to you in thanksgiving, yet all too conscious of our pride and vanity which has caused your world to become polluted.

Guide and govern your Church, that she may teach the world of your love for us in the beauty of the created order. We pray for Christian projects whose aim is to enhance our appreciation of God's world ....: O Lord our Governor,
your name is glorious in all the world.

You have given us dominion over your creation, yet we have misused that power; we have turned rich valleys into deserts and destroyed the habitats of living creatures. Have mercy on our carelessness and wilful destruction, and enable us to repair the damage we are causing ....: O Lord our Governor,
your name is glorious in all the world.

You have set in place the moon and the stars, and the heavens are the work of your fingers. Forgive us for the times when our curiosity has turned to exploitation: O Lord our Governor,
your name is glorious in all the world.

You have created a world rich with natural resources, yet we abuse that generosity and exploit the vulnerable. Stir in our hearts a desire to work for those who are poor and unjustly treated ....: O Lord our Governor,
your name is glorious in all the world.

May the departed enjoy the peaceful harmony of heaven, where there is the joy of eternal bliss with you ....: O Lord our Governor,
your name is glorious in all the world.

Rogation Days

We come to you, O Lord, with thankful hearts, for you are generous and you pour down your graciousness upon us.

Give your Church the gift of humility, that our work done in secret will gain a heavenly reward: give us our daily bread, O Lord,
teach us to be thankful.

Let your love and generosity be imitated by those who hold authority in our world. May your generous and bountiful harvests be justly distributed: give us our daily bread, O Lord,
teach us to be thankful.

Bless and guide our community .... Enable us to reach out in love and charity to those who are deprived of the essentials of daily living: give us our daily bread, O Lord,
teach us to be thankful.

Help us care for the sick .... and for those who live in the shadow of poverty and despair. Mould our hearts to your will: give us our daily bread, O Lord,
teach us to be thankful.

May the faithful departed share in the joys of your eternal presence, for they have kept the faith and run the course ....:
give us our daily bread, O Lord,
teach us to be thankful.

Mission and Evangelism

Lord God, you have given us authority to preach your word to the world. Give us the needful gifts of your Holy Spirit, that we may bear witness to your love.

We rest in the confidence of your presence. Enable us, your Church, to preach the word to a confused and distracted world ....: praise the Lord, all you nations,
praise him all you peoples.

The world you have made is staggering in its beauty, yet so often we betray that beauty with violence and war. Give wisdom to all in authority, that they may witness to the abiding presence of your love: praise the Lord, all you nations,
praise him all you peoples.

Bless and direct our own efforts to witness to your love in the world .... Bless this parish and the connections we have fostered .... Enable us to teach the faith with love, generosity and patience: praise the Lord, all you nations,
praise him all you peoples.

Bless those who witness to your love in our hospitals, nursing homes and hospices .... May their constancy reveal to those in their care your continuing presence: praise the Lord, all you nations,
praise him all you peoples.

May the faithful departed be with you for ever, for they were joyful witnesses to your love on earth ....: praise the Lord, all you nations,
praise him all you peoples.

Unity

It is a good and pleasant thing to live together in unity, so we come to you in prayer, asking your blessings upon us as we seek your will in our Church and world today.

We pray for all Christians. Forge us into unity, mend our way-wardness and forgive us the disunity we have sown through our lack of vision ....: keep us in your name,
that we may be one.

Unite your peoples throughout the world. Help us work to-gether in serving the common good, that all your children may flourish ....: keep us in your name,
that we may be one.

We pray for our Christian partnerships here in N .... May your will govern our thinking, and forgive us the times when we have indulged in party spirit and faction: keep us in your name,
that we may be one.

We pray for Christians who face persecution. Enable us to work for a greater understanding among all peoples: keep us in your name,
that we may be one.

We give thanks to God for all the faithful departed. As they have ended their earthly exile bring them to that heavenly homeland, where we shall all unite around the throne: keep us in your name,
that we may be one.

The Peace of the World

In the midst of our pain and anguish we cry to you, for you alone are our strength and peace.

Shower upon your Church the gift of peace .... Fill us with mutual love, and enable us to witness to your grace in a crooked and twisted world: show us the paths of peace,
so that your will may reign.

Fill your world with a spirit of compassion. We pray for ....
Transform the hearts of all who pursue war and are indifferent to the suffering of innocents ....: show us the paths of peace,
so that your will may reign.

Give grace and comfort to families. Unite this community .... Help us together to sow seeds of love and peace in the hearts of your children: show us the paths of peace,
so that your will may reign.

Pour your healing balm upon those who are victims of war: the sick, the wounded and the mentally scarred .... Bless all agencies who strive to end the cycle of war and hatred: show us the paths of peace,
so that your will may reign.

Gather into your most sacred heart all who have died in conflict, whose deaths were sudden and unprepared. Give them your peace: show us the paths of peace,
so that your will may reign.

Social Justice

We come to you, O Lord   promised to
hear the cries of your chil   distress.

Guide your Church in the v   may reach
out in love and gentleness t   oice in our
society .... Give us grace   nd love: in
your mercy hear us,
and let our cry come to you.

Give courage to those individuals and agencies who speak out
against the abuse of human rights in our world .... Enable
us to listen and to support them: in your mercy hear us,
and let our cry come to you.

Help us respond to the call of the gospel in this parish ....
Strengthen us to care for those who are vulnerable and in need
..........: in your mercy hear us,
and let our cry come to you.

Bless those who are unable to provide for their families ....
and for those who are unable to provide for the basic necessi-
ties of life .... Pour upon them, O Lord, your grace, and
kindle in us the desire to serve you in them: in your mercy
hear us,
and let our cry come to you.

Give eternal life to the faithful departed. We remember in particular those whose lives were characterized by love and service
in imitation of their Lord and Saviour ....: in your mercy
hear us,
and let our cry come to you.

Ministry

As servants of God we come before you to offer our prayers. Pour your Spirit into our hearts, that we may give ourselves in love and service.

Guide and inspire all who are entrusted with the ministry of word and sacrament .... Bless all who minister to the needs of this parish, that we may fulfil your calling to us: Lord, bless your people,
and fill us with your Holy Spirit.

Guide and bless those who hold positions of authority. We pray for our own rulers .... Help us respond to the challenges that God holds out for us: Lord, bless your people,
and fill us with your Holy Spirit.

Strengthen the gift of faith in us so that we may be responsive to your call for us in this parish .... Enable us to live faithfully under your will: Lord, bless your people,
and fill us with your Holy Spirit.

To be used when Ember lists are published

Bless all those who are to be ordained to the diaconate and priesthood .... Guide them in their ministry and inspire them to be faithful and constant in service: Lord, bless your people,
and fill us with your Holy Spirit.

Hold in your special care those who feel that their calling has been frustrated and denied .... Strengthen their hearts and wills, that they may respond to this disappointment with love: Lord, bless your people,
and fill us with your Holy Spirit.

We give thanks for all faithful ministers of the gospel who have now gone to their rest ………. They serve for ever around the altar of the most high: Lord, bless your people,
and fill us with your Holy Spirit.

Healing

We bring before you, O Lord Jesus Christ, the needs of those who cry to you for healing.

Guide your Church in her healing ministry ………. We pray for our hospitals and hospital chaplains ………. We give thanks for the ministry, skill and dedication of those who are called to care for the sick ……….: the fruit of the tree of life will be our food,
the leaves will be for healing.

We live in a world in need of your healing grace. Bring healing to our torn and divided world ………. Feed the hungry and fill your children with hope for their futures: the fruit of the tree of life will be our food,
the leaves will be for healing.

Guide and encourage all who are involved in the healing ministry of your Church; in particular we pray for this church ………. Enable us to bring in your kingdom where there will be no more pain but life everlasting: the fruit of the tree of life will be our food,
the leaves will be for healing.

Protect the sick and the needy ………. May your will be fulfilled in their lives: the fruit of the tree of life will be our food,
the leaves will be for healing.

Grant eternal rest to the departed .... May they share in the eternal joys of heaven, free from pain and sorrow. Bring comfort and healing to those who mourn: the fruit of the tree of life will be our food,
the leaves will be for healing.